Buy The Bay Books © Copyright 2021. All Rights Reserved.

If found please return this

WALL CLIMBING JOURNAL

to:

_____

_____

LOCATION		DATE			
CLIMB TYPE					
CLIMB HEIGHT		/ /			

TEMPERATURE		DIFFICULTY RATING	1	2	3	4	5
HUMIDITY							
WEATHER CONDITION	☀ ☁ ❄ ⛈ 💨	TIME OF YEAR	🌷 ☀ 🍃 ❄				

START TIME	🕐	CLIMB CHECKLIST	
END TIME		☐ CLIMB ROPE	☐ CARABINER
TOTAL TIME TO TOP	⬆	☐ BELAY DEVICE	☐ HELMET
		☐ QUICKDRAW	☐ HARNESS

CLIMB PARTNER(S)

MILESTONES ACHIEVED	AIMS FOR NEXT CLIMB

ROUTE TAKEN	BETA NOTES

FURTHER OBSERVATIONS

_____
_____
_____

LOCATION		DATE	
CLIMB TYPE			
CLIMB HEIGHT		/ /	

TEMPERATURE		DIFFICULTY RATING	1 2 3 4 5
HUMIDITY			
WEATHER CONDITION	☀ ☁ ❄ ⛈ 〰	TIME OF YEAR	🌷 ☀ 🍃 ❄

START TIME	🕐	CLIMB CHECKLIST	
END TIME		☐ CLIMB ROPE	☐ CARABINER
TOTAL TIME TO TOP	⬆	☐ BELAY DEVICE	☐ HELMET
		☐ QUICKDRAW	☐ HARNESS

CLIMB PARTNER(S)

MILESTONES ACHIEVED	AIMS FOR NEXT CLIMB

ROUTE TAKEN	BETA NOTES

FURTHER OBSERVATIONS

LOCATION		DATE	
CLIMB TYPE			
CLIMB HEIGHT		/ /	

TEMPERATURE		DIFFICULTY RATING	1 2 3 4 5
HUMIDITY			
WEATHER CONDITION	☀ ☂ ❄ ⛈ 💨	TIME OF YEAR	🌷 ☀ 🍃 ❄

START TIME	🕐	CLIMB CHECKLIST	
END TIME		☐ CLIMB ROPE	☐ CARABINER
TOTAL TIME TO TOP	⬆	☐ BELAY DEVICE	☐ HELMET
		☐ QUICKDRAW	☐ HARNESS

CLIMB PARTNER(S)

MILESTONES ACHIEVED | AIMS FOR NEXT CLIMB

ROUTE TAKEN | BETA NOTES

FURTHER OBSERVATIONS

LOCATION		DATE		
CLIMB TYPE				
CLIMB HEIGHT		/ /		

TEMPERATURE		DIFFICULTY RATING	1	2	3	4	5
HUMIDITY							

WEATHER CONDITION	☀ ☁ ❄ ⛈ 🌬	TIME OF YEAR	🌷 ☀ 🍃 ❄

START TIME	🕐	CLIMB CHECKLIST	
END TIME		☐ CLIMB ROPE	☐ CARABINER
TOTAL TIME TO TOP	⬆	☐ BELAY DEVICE	☐ HELMET
		☐ QUICKDRAW	☐ HARNESS

CLIMB PARTNER(S)

MILESTONES ACHIEVED	AIMS FOR NEXT CLIMB

ROUTE TAKEN	BETA NOTES

FURTHER OBSERVATIONS

LOCATION		DATE				
CLIMB TYPE						
CLIMB HEIGHT		/ /				
TEMPERATURE		DIFFICULTY RATING	1	2	3	4	5
HUMIDITY						
WEATHER CONDITION	☀ ☁ ❄ ⛈ 🌬	TIME OF YEAR	🌷 ☀ 🍃 ❄			
START TIME	🕐	CLIMB CHECKLIST				
END TIME		☐ CLIMB ROPE	☐ CARABINER			
TOTAL TIME TO TOP	⬆	☐ BELAY DEVICE	☐ HELMET			
		☐ QUICKDRAW	☐ HARNESS			

CLIMB PARTNER(S)

MILESTONES ACHIEVED | AIMS FOR NEXT CLIMB

ROUTE TAKEN | BETA NOTES

FURTHER OBSERVATIONS

LOCATION		DATE				
CLIMB TYPE		/ /				
CLIMB HEIGHT						
TEMPERATURE		DIFFICULTY RATING	1	2	3	4	5
HUMIDITY						
WEATHER CONDITION	☀ ☁ ❄ ⛈ 💨	TIME OF YEAR	🌷 ☀ 🍁 ❄			

START TIME		CLIMB CHECKLIST	
END TIME	🕐	☐ CLIMB ROPE	☐ CARABINER
TOTAL TIME TO TOP	⬆	☐ BELAY DEVICE	☐ HELMET
		☐ QUICKDRAW	☐ HARNESS

CLIMB PARTNER(S)

MILESTONES ACHIEVED	AIMS FOR NEXT CLIMB

ROUTE TAKEN	BETA NOTES

FURTHER OBSERVATIONS

LOCATION		DATE			
CLIMB TYPE					
CLIMB HEIGHT		/ /			

TEMPERATURE		DIFFICULTY RATING	1	2	3	4	5
HUMIDITY							

WEATHER CONDITION	☀ ☁ ❄ ⛈ 🌬	TIME OF YEAR	🌷 ☀ 🍃 ❄

START TIME		CLIMB CHECKLIST	
END TIME	🕐	☐ CLIMB ROPE	☐ CARABINER
TOTAL TIME TO TOP	⬆	☐ BELAY DEVICE	☐ HELMET
		☐ QUICKDRAW	☐ HARNESS

CLIMB PARTNER(S)

MILESTONES ACHIEVED	AIMS FOR NEXT CLIMB

ROUTE TAKEN	BETA NOTES

FURTHER OBSERVATIONS

_____
_____
_____

LOCATION		DATE	
CLIMB TYPE			
CLIMB HEIGHT		/ /	

TEMPERATURE		DIFFICULTY RATING	1 2 3 4 5
HUMIDITY			

WEATHER CONDITION	☀ ☁ ❄ ⛈ 💨	TIME OF YEAR	🌷 ☀ 🍃 ❄

START TIME	🕐	CLIMB CHECKLIST	
END TIME		☐ CLIMB ROPE	☐ CARABINER
TOTAL TIME TO TOP	⬆	☐ BELAY DEVICE	☐ HELMET
		☐ QUICKDRAW	☐ HARNESS

CLIMB PARTNER(S)

MILESTONES ACHIEVED	AIMS FOR NEXT CLIMB

ROUTE TAKEN	BETA NOTES

FURTHER OBSERVATIONS

LOCATION		DATE		
CLIMB TYPE				
CLIMB HEIGHT		/ /		

TEMPERATURE		DIFFICULTY RATING	1	2	3	4	5
HUMIDITY							

WEATHER CONDITION	☀ ☁ ❄ ⛈ 🌬	TIME OF YEAR	🌷 ☀ 🍃 ❄

START TIME	🕐	CLIMB CHECKLIST	
END TIME		☐ CLIMB ROPE	☐ CARABINER
TOTAL TIME TO TOP	⬆	☐ BELAY DEVICE	☐ HELMET
		☐ QUICKDRAW	☐ HARNESS

CLIMB PARTNER(S)

MILESTONES ACHIEVED	AIMS FOR NEXT CLIMB

ROUTE TAKEN	BETA NOTES

FURTHER OBSERVATIONS

___
___

LOCATION		DATE				
CLIMB TYPE		/ /				
CLIMB HEIGHT						

TEMPERATURE		DIFFICULTY RATING	1	2	3	4	5
HUMIDITY							
WEATHER CONDITION	☀ ☁ ❄ ⛈ 🌬	TIME OF YEAR	🌷	☀	🍁	❄	

START TIME	🕐	CLIMB CHECKLIST	
END TIME		☐ CLIMB ROPE	☐ CARABINER
TOTAL TIME TO TOP	⬆	☐ BELAY DEVICE	☐ HELMET
		☐ QUICKDRAW	☐ HARNESS

CLIMB PARTNER(S)

MILESTONES ACHIEVED | AIMS FOR NEXT CLIMB

ROUTE TAKEN | BETA NOTES

FURTHER OBSERVATIONS

_____
_____
_____

LOCATION		DATE	
CLIMB TYPE			
CLIMB HEIGHT		/ /	

TEMPERATURE		DIFFICULTY RATING	1 2 3 4 5
HUMIDITY			
WEATHER CONDITION	☀ ☁ ❄ ⛈ 🌬	TIME OF YEAR	🌷 ☀ 🍃 ❄
START TIME	🕐	**CLIMB CHECKLIST**	
END TIME		☐ CLIMB ROPE	☐ CARABINER
TOTAL TIME TO TOP	⬆	☐ BELAY DEVICE	☐ HELMET
		☐ QUICKDRAW	☐ HARNESS

CLIMB PARTNER(S)

MILESTONES ACHIEVED | AIMS FOR NEXT CLIMB

ROUTE TAKEN | BETA NOTES

FURTHER OBSERVATIONS

_____
_____
_____

LOCATION		DATE	
CLIMB TYPE			
CLIMB HEIGHT			

TEMPERATURE		DIFFICULTY RATING	1 2 3 4 5
HUMIDITY			
WEATHER CONDITION	☀ ☁ ❄ ⛈ 🌬	TIME OF YEAR	🌷 ☀ 🍃 ❄

START TIME	🕐	**CLIMB CHECKLIST**	
END TIME		☐ CLIMB ROPE	☐ CARABINER
TOTAL TIME TO TOP	⬆	☐ BELAY DEVICE	☐ HELMET
		☐ QUICKDRAW	☐ HARNESS

CLIMB PARTNER(S)

MILESTONES ACHIEVED	AIMS FOR NEXT CLIMB

ROUTE TAKEN	BETA NOTES

FURTHER OBSERVATIONS

LOCATION		DATE		
CLIMB TYPE				
CLIMB HEIGHT		/	/	

TEMPERATURE		DIFFICULTY RATING	1	2	3	4	5
HUMIDITY							

WEATHER CONDITION	☀ ☁ ❄ ⛈ 💨	TIME OF YEAR	🌷 ☀ 🍃 ❄

START TIME	🕐	CLIMB CHECKLIST	
END TIME		☐ CLIMB ROPE	☐ CARABINER
TOTAL TIME TO TOP	⬆	☐ BELAY DEVICE	☐ HELMET
		☐ QUICKDRAW	☐ HARNESS

CLIMB PARTNER(S)

MILESTONES ACHIEVED	AIMS FOR NEXT CLIMB

ROUTE TAKEN	BETA NOTES

FURTHER OBSERVATIONS

_____

_____

LOCATION		DATE	
CLIMB TYPE			
CLIMB HEIGHT		/ /	

TEMPERATURE		DIFFICULTY RATING	1 2 3 4 5
HUMIDITY			

WEATHER CONDITION	☀ ☁ ❄ ⛈ 🌬	TIME OF YEAR	🌷 ☀ 🍃 ❄

START TIME	🕐	**CLIMB CHECKLIST**	
END TIME		☐ CLIMB ROPE	☐ CARABINER
TOTAL TIME TO TOP	⬆	☐ BELAY DEVICE	☐ HELMET
		☐ QUICKDRAW	☐ HARNESS

CLIMB PARTNER(S)

MILESTONES ACHIEVED	AIMS FOR NEXT CLIMB

ROUTE TAKEN	BETA NOTES

FURTHER OBSERVATIONS

LOCATION		DATE	
CLIMB TYPE			
CLIMB HEIGHT		/ /	

TEMPERATURE		DIFFICULTY RATING	1 2 3 4 5
HUMIDITY			

WEATHER CONDITION	☀ ☔ ❄ ⛈ 🌬	TIME OF YEAR	🌷 ☀ 🍃 ❄

START TIME	🕐	CLIMB CHECKLIST	
END TIME		☐ CLIMB ROPE	☐ CARABINER
TOTAL TIME TO TOP	⬆	☐ BELAY DEVICE	☐ HELMET
		☐ QUICKDRAW	☐ HARNESS

CLIMB PARTNER(S)

MILESTONES ACHIEVED | AIMS FOR NEXT CLIMB

ROUTE TAKEN | BETA NOTES

FURTHER OBSERVATIONS

___
___

LOCATION		DATE	
CLIMB TYPE			
CLIMB HEIGHT			

TEMPERATURE		DIFFICULTY RATING	1	2	3	4	5
HUMIDITY							

WEATHER CONDITION	☀ ☁ ❄ ⚡ 💨	TIME OF YEAR	🌷 ☀ 🍃 ❄

START TIME	🕐	CLIMB CHECKLIST	
END TIME		☐ CLIMB ROPE	☐ CARABINER
TOTAL TIME TO TOP	⬆	☐ BELAY DEVICE	☐ HELMET
		☐ QUICKDRAW	☐ HARNESS

CLIMB PARTNER(S)

MILESTONES ACHIEVED	AIMS FOR NEXT CLIMB

ROUTE TAKEN	BETA NOTES

FURTHER OBSERVATIONS

LOCATION		DATE		
CLIMB TYPE				
CLIMB HEIGHT		/ /		

TEMPERATURE		DIFFICULTY RATING	1 2 3 4 5
HUMIDITY			
WEATHER CONDITION	☀ 🌧 ❄ ⛈ 💨	TIME OF YEAR	🌷 ☀ 🍃 ❄
START TIME	🕐	**CLIMB CHECKLIST**	
END TIME		☐ CLIMB ROPE ☐ CARABINER	
TOTAL TIME TO TOP	⬆	☐ BELAY DEVICE ☐ HELMET	
		☐ QUICKDRAW ☐ HARNESS	

CLIMB PARTNER(S)

MILESTONES ACHIEVED | AIMS FOR NEXT CLIMB

ROUTE TAKEN | BETA NOTES

FURTHER OBSERVATIONS

LOCATION						DATE				
CLIMB TYPE										
CLIMB HEIGHT										

TEMPERATURE		DIFFICULTY RATING	1	2	3	4	5
HUMIDITY							
WEATHER CONDITION	☀ ☁ ❄ ⛈ 💨	TIME OF YEAR	🌷 ☀ 🍃 ❄				

START TIME	🕐	CLIMB CHECKLIST	
END TIME		☐ CLIMB ROPE	☐ CARABINER
TOTAL TIME TO TOP	⬆	☐ BELAY DEVICE	☐ HELMET
		☐ QUICKDRAW	☐ HARNESS

CLIMB PARTNER(S)

MILESTONES ACHIEVED | AIMS FOR NEXT CLIMB

ROUTE TAKEN | BETA NOTES

FURTHER OBSERVATIONS

___
___
___

LOCATION		DATE				
CLIMB TYPE						
CLIMB HEIGHT		/ /				

TEMPERATURE		DIFFICULTY RATING	1	2	3	4	5
HUMIDITY							

WEATHER CONDITION	☀ ☁ ❄ ⛈ 💨	TIME OF YEAR	🌷 ☀ 🍃 ❄

START TIME	🕐	CLIMB CHECKLIST	
END TIME		☐ CLIMB ROPE	☐ CARABINER
TOTAL TIME TO TOP	⬆	☐ BELAY DEVICE	☐ HELMET
		☐ QUICKDRAW	☐ HARNESS

CLIMB PARTNER(S)

MILESTONES ACHIEVED	AIMS FOR NEXT CLIMB

ROUTE TAKEN	BETA NOTES

FURTHER OBSERVATIONS

LOCATION		DATE	
CLIMB TYPE			
CLIMB HEIGHT		/ /	

TEMPERATURE		DIFFICULTY RATING	1 2 3 4 5
HUMIDITY			

WEATHER CONDITION	☀ ☁ ❄ ⛈ 🌬	TIME OF YEAR	🌷 ☀ 🍃 ❄

START TIME		**CLIMB CHECKLIST**	
END TIME		☐ CLIMB ROPE	☐ CARABINER
TOTAL TIME TO TOP	⬆	☐ BELAY DEVICE	☐ HELMET
		☐ QUICKDRAW	☐ HARNESS

CLIMB PARTNER(S)

MILESTONES ACHIEVED | AIMS FOR NEXT CLIMB

ROUTE TAKEN | BETA NOTES

FURTHER OBSERVATIONS

LOCATION		DATE	
CLIMB TYPE			
CLIMB HEIGHT		/ /	

TEMPERATURE		DIFFICULTY RATING	1 2 3 4 5
HUMIDITY			
WEATHER CONDITION	☀ ☔ ❄ ⛈ 💨	TIME OF YEAR	🌷 ☀ 🍃 ❄

START TIME	🕐	**CLIMB CHECKLIST**	
END TIME		☐ CLIMB ROPE	☐ CARABINER
TOTAL TIME TO TOP	⬆	☐ BELAY DEVICE	☐ HELMET
		☐ QUICKDRAW	☐ HARNESS

CLIMB PARTNER(S)

MILESTONES ACHIEVED	AIMS FOR NEXT CLIMB

ROUTE TAKEN	BETA NOTES

FURTHER OBSERVATIONS

LOCATION		DATE	
CLIMB TYPE			
CLIMB HEIGHT		/ /	

TEMPERATURE		DIFFICULTY RATING	1	2	3	4	5
HUMIDITY							

WEATHER CONDITION	☀ ☁ ❄ ⚡ 🌬	TIME OF YEAR	🌷 ☀ 🍃 ❄

START TIME	🕐	CLIMB CHECKLIST	
END TIME		☐ CLIMB ROPE	☐ CARABINER
TOTAL TIME TO TOP	⬆	☐ BELAY DEVICE	☐ HELMET
		☐ QUICKDRAW	☐ HARNESS

CLIMB PARTNER(S)

MILESTONES ACHIEVED	AIMS FOR NEXT CLIMB

ROUTE TAKEN	BETA NOTES

FURTHER OBSERVATIONS

LOCATION		DATE				
CLIMB TYPE						
CLIMB HEIGHT		/ /				

TEMPERATURE		DIFFICULTY RATING	1	2	3	4	5
HUMIDITY							

WEATHER CONDITION		TIME OF YEAR	

START TIME		CLIMB CHECKLIST	
END TIME		☐ CLIMB ROPE	☐ CARABINER
TOTAL TIME TO TOP		☐ BELAY DEVICE	☐ HELMET
		☐ QUICKDRAW	☐ HARNESS

CLIMB PARTNER(S)

MILESTONES ACHIEVED	AIMS FOR NEXT CLIMB

ROUTE TAKEN	BETA NOTES

FURTHER OBSERVATIONS

LOCATION		DATE	
CLIMB TYPE			
CLIMB HEIGHT			

TEMPERATURE		DIFFICULTY RATING	1 2 3 4 5
HUMIDITY			
WEATHER CONDITION	☀ ☁ ❄ ⛈ 💨	TIME OF YEAR	🌳 ☀ 🍁 ❄

START TIME	🕐	CLIMB CHECKLIST	
END TIME		☐ CLIMB ROPE	☐ CARABINER
TOTAL TIME TO TOP	⬆	☐ BELAY DEVICE	☐ HELMET
		☐ QUICKDRAW	☐ HARNESS

CLIMB PARTNER(S)

MILESTONES ACHIEVED	AIMS FOR NEXT CLIMB

ROUTE TAKEN	BETA NOTES

FURTHER OBSERVATIONS

LOCATION		DATE
CLIMB TYPE		
CLIMB HEIGHT		/ /

TEMPERATURE		DIFFICULTY RATING	1	2	3	4	5
HUMIDITY							

WEATHER CONDITION	☀ ☁ ❄ ⛈ 〰	TIME OF YEAR	🌷 ☀ 🍁 ❄

START TIME	🕐	CLIMB CHECKLIST	
END TIME		☐ CLIMB ROPE	☐ CARABINER
TOTAL TIME TO TOP	⬆	☐ BELAY DEVICE	☐ HELMET
		☐ QUICKDRAW	☐ HARNESS

CLIMB PARTNER(S)

MILESTONES ACHIEVED	AIMS FOR NEXT CLIMB

ROUTE TAKEN	BETA NOTES

FURTHER OBSERVATIONS

LOCATION		DATE				
CLIMB TYPE						
CLIMB HEIGHT		/ /				

TEMPERATURE		DIFFICULTY RATING	1	2	3	4	5
HUMIDITY							

WEATHER CONDITION	☀ ☔ ❄ ⛈ 💨	TIME OF YEAR	🌷 ☀ 🍁 ❄

START TIME	🕐	CLIMB CHECKLIST	
END TIME		☐ CLIMB ROPE	☐ CARABINER
TOTAL TIME TO TOP	⬆	☐ BELAY DEVICE	☐ HELMET
		☐ QUICKDRAW	☐ HARNESS

CLIMB PARTNER(S)

MILESTONES ACHIEVED	AIMS FOR NEXT CLIMB

ROUTE TAKEN	BETA NOTES

FURTHER OBSERVATIONS

LOCATION		DATE				
CLIMB TYPE						
CLIMB HEIGHT		/ /				

TEMPERATURE		DIFFICULTY RATING	1	2	3	4	5
HUMIDITY							

WEATHER CONDITION	☀ ☁ ❄ ⚡ 💨	TIME OF YEAR	🌷 ☀ 🍃 ❄

START TIME	🕐	CLIMB CHECKLIST	
END TIME		☐ CLIMB ROPE	☐ CARABINER
TOTAL TIME TO TOP	⬆	☐ BELAY DEVICE	☐ HELMET
		☐ QUICKDRAW	☐ HARNESS

CLIMB PARTNER(S)

MILESTONES ACHIEVED	AIMS FOR NEXT CLIMB

ROUTE TAKEN	BETA NOTES

FURTHER OBSERVATIONS

LOCATION		DATE	
CLIMB TYPE			
CLIMB HEIGHT		/ /	

TEMPERATURE		DIFFICULTY RATING	1 2 3 4 5
HUMIDITY			
WEATHER CONDITION	☀ ☂ ❄ ⛈ 🌬	TIME OF YEAR	🌷 ☀ 🍃 ❄

START TIME	🕐	CLIMB CHECKLIST	
END TIME		☐ CLIMB ROPE	☐ CARABINER
TOTAL TIME TO TOP	⬆	☐ BELAY DEVICE	☐ HELMET
		☐ QUICKDRAW	☐ HARNESS

CLIMB PARTNER(S)

MILESTONES ACHIEVED	AIMS FOR NEXT CLIMB

ROUTE TAKEN	BETA NOTES

FURTHER OBSERVATIONS

___
___
___

LOCATION		DATE	
CLIMB TYPE			
CLIMB HEIGHT		/ /	

TEMPERATURE		DIFFICULTY RATING	1 2 3 4 5
HUMIDITY			
WEATHER CONDITION	☀ ☁ ❄ ⛈ 💨	TIME OF YEAR	🌷 ☀ 🍃 ❄
START TIME	🕐	**CLIMB CHECKLIST**	
END TIME		☐ CLIMB ROPE ☐ CARABINER	
TOTAL TIME TO TOP	⬆	☐ BELAY DEVICE ☐ HELMET	
		☐ QUICKDRAW ☐ HARNESS	

CLIMB PARTNER(S)

MILESTONES ACHIEVED | AIMS FOR NEXT CLIMB

ROUTE TAKEN | BETA NOTES

FURTHER OBSERVATIONS

_____
_____
_____

LOCATION		DATE				
CLIMB TYPE						
CLIMB HEIGHT		/ /				

TEMPERATURE		DIFFICULTY RATING	1	2	3	4	5
HUMIDITY							
WEATHER CONDITION	☀ ☁ ❄ ⛈ 🌬	TIME OF YEAR	🌷 ☀ 🍃 ❄				
START TIME	🕐	**CLIMB CHECKLIST**					
END TIME		☐ CLIMB ROPE	☐ CARABINER				
TOTAL TIME TO TOP	⬆	☐ BELAY DEVICE	☐ HELMET				
		☐ QUICKDRAW	☐ HARNESS				

CLIMB PARTNER(S)

MILESTONES ACHIEVED	AIMS FOR NEXT CLIMB

ROUTE TAKEN	BETA NOTES

FURTHER OBSERVATIONS

LOCATION		DATE		
CLIMB TYPE				
CLIMB HEIGHT		/ /		

TEMPERATURE		DIFFICULTY RATING	1	2	3	4	5
HUMIDITY							

WEATHER CONDITION	☀ ☁ ❄ ⛈ 💨	TIME OF YEAR	🌷 ☀ 🍃 ❄

START TIME	🕐	CLIMB CHECKLIST	
END TIME		☐ CLIMB ROPE	☐ CARABINER
TOTAL TIME TO TOP	⬆	☐ BELAY DEVICE	☐ HELMET
		☐ QUICKDRAW	☐ HARNESS

CLIMB PARTNER(S)

MILESTONES ACHIEVED	AIMS FOR NEXT CLIMB

ROUTE TAKEN	BETA NOTES

FURTHER OBSERVATIONS

_____
_____
_____

LOCATION		DATE	
CLIMB TYPE			
CLIMB HEIGHT		/ /	

TEMPERATURE		DIFFICULTY RATING	1 2 3 4 5	
HUMIDITY				
WEATHER CONDITION	☀ ☁ ❄ ⛈ 🌬	TIME OF YEAR	🌷 ☀ 🍃 ❄	
START TIME	🕐	**CLIMB CHECKLIST**		
END TIME		☐ CLIMB ROPE	☐ CARABINER	
TOTAL TIME TO TOP	⬆	☐ BELAY DEVICE	☐ HELMET	
		☐ QUICKDRAW	☐ HARNESS	

CLIMB PARTNER(S)

MILESTONES ACHIEVED	AIMS FOR NEXT CLIMB

ROUTE TAKEN	BETA NOTES

FURTHER OBSERVATIONS

LOCATION		DATE	
CLIMB TYPE			
CLIMB HEIGHT		/ /	

TEMPERATURE		DIFFICULTY RATING	1 2 3 4 5
HUMIDITY			
WEATHER CONDITION	☀ ☂ ❄ ⛈ 〰	TIME OF YEAR	🌷 ☀ 🍁 ❄
START TIME	🕐	**CLIMB CHECKLIST**	
END TIME		☐ CLIMB ROPE ☐ CARABINER	
TOTAL TIME TO TOP	⬆	☐ BELAY DEVICE ☐ HELMET	
		☐ QUICKDRAW ☐ HARNESS	

CLIMB PARTNER(S)

MILESTONES ACHIEVED	AIMS FOR NEXT CLIMB

ROUTE TAKEN	BETA NOTES

FURTHER OBSERVATIONS

___
___
___

LOCATION		DATE		
CLIMB TYPE				
CLIMB HEIGHT		/ /		

TEMPERATURE		DIFFICULTY RATING	1	2	3	4	5
HUMIDITY							

WEATHER CONDITION	☀ ☁ ❄ ⛈ 💨	TIME OF YEAR	🌷 ☀ 🍃 ❄

START TIME	🕐	CLIMB CHECKLIST	
END TIME		☐ CLIMB ROPE	☐ CARABINER
TOTAL TIME TO TOP	⬆	☐ BELAY DEVICE	☐ HELMET
		☐ QUICKDRAW	☐ HARNESS

CLIMB PARTNER(S)

MILESTONES ACHIEVED	AIMS FOR NEXT CLIMB

ROUTE TAKEN	BETA NOTES

FURTHER OBSERVATIONS

LOCATION						DATE		
CLIMB TYPE								
CLIMB HEIGHT								

TEMPERATURE						DIFFICULTY RATING	1	2	3	4	5
HUMIDITY											
WEATHER CONDITION	☀	☁🌧	❄	⛈	💨	TIME OF YEAR	🌷	☀	🍃	❄	
START TIME	🕐					**CLIMB CHECKLIST**					
END TIME						☐ CLIMB ROPE	☐ CARABINER				
TOTAL TIME TO TOP	⬆					☐ BELAY DEVICE	☐ HELMET				
						☐ QUICKDRAW	☐ HARNESS				

CLIMB PARTNER(S)

MILESTONES ACHIEVED	AIMS FOR NEXT CLIMB

ROUTE TAKEN	BETA NOTES

FURTHER OBSERVATIONS

LOCATION		DATE				
CLIMB TYPE						
CLIMB HEIGHT		/ /				

TEMPERATURE		DIFFICULTY RATING	1	2	3	4	5
HUMIDITY							
WEATHER CONDITION	☀ ☁ ❄ ⚡ 💨	TIME OF YEAR	🌷 ☀ 🍁 ❄				

START TIME	🕐	CLIMB CHECKLIST	
END TIME		☐ CLIMB ROPE	☐ CARABINER
TOTAL TIME TO TOP	⬆	☐ BELAY DEVICE	☐ HELMET
		☐ QUICKDRAW	☐ HARNESS

CLIMB PARTNER(S)

MILESTONES ACHIEVED	AIMS FOR NEXT CLIMB

ROUTE TAKEN	BETA NOTES

FURTHER OBSERVATIONS

LOCATION		DATE				
CLIMB TYPE						
CLIMB HEIGHT		/ /				

TEMPERATURE		DIFFICULTY RATING	1	2	3	4	5
HUMIDITY							
WEATHER CONDITION	☀ ☁ ❄ ⛈ 💨	TIME OF YEAR	🌷 ☀ 🍃 ❄				

START TIME	🕐	CLIMB CHECKLIST	
END TIME		☐ CLIMB ROPE	☐ CARABINER
TOTAL TIME TO TOP	⬆	☐ BELAY DEVICE	☐ HELMET
		☐ QUICKDRAW	☐ HARNESS

CLIMB PARTNER(S)

MILESTONES ACHIEVED	AIMS FOR NEXT CLIMB

ROUTE TAKEN	BETA NOTES

FURTHER OBSERVATIONS

_____

_____

_____

LOCATION		DATE				
CLIMB TYPE						
CLIMB HEIGHT		/ /				

TEMPERATURE		DIFFICULTY RATING	1	2	3	4	5
HUMIDITY							

WEATHER CONDITION	☀ ☁ ❄ ⛈ 💨	TIME OF YEAR	🌷 ☀ 🍃 ❄

START TIME	🕐	CLIMB CHECKLIST	
END TIME		☐ CLIMB ROPE	☐ CARABINER
TOTAL TIME TO TOP	⬆	☐ BELAY DEVICE	☐ HELMET
		☐ QUICKDRAW	☐ HARNESS

CLIMB PARTNER(S)

MILESTONES ACHIEVED | AIMS FOR NEXT CLIMB

ROUTE TAKEN | BETA NOTES

FURTHER OBSERVATIONS

LOCATION		DATE	
CLIMB TYPE			
CLIMB HEIGHT		/ /	

TEMPERATURE		DIFFICULTY RATING	1 2 3 4 5
HUMIDITY			
WEATHER CONDITION	☀ ☁ ❄ ⛈ 〰	TIME OF YEAR	🌷 ☀ 🍃 ❄

START TIME	🕐	CLIMB CHECKLIST	
END TIME		☐ CLIMB ROPE	☐ CARABINER
TOTAL TIME TO TOP	⬆	☐ BELAY DEVICE	☐ HELMET
		☐ QUICKDRAW	☐ HARNESS

CLIMB PARTNER(S)

MILESTONES ACHIEVED	AIMS FOR NEXT CLIMB

ROUTE TAKEN	BETA NOTES

FURTHER OBSERVATIONS

LOCATION		DATE				
CLIMB TYPE						
CLIMB HEIGHT		/ /				

TEMPERATURE		DIFFICULTY RATING	1	2	3	4	5
HUMIDITY							

WEATHER CONDITION	☀ ☁ ❄ ⛈ 💨	TIME OF YEAR	🌷 ☀ 🍃 ❄

START TIME	🕐	CLIMB CHECKLIST	
END TIME		☐ CLIMB ROPE	☐ CARABINER
TOTAL TIME TO TOP	⬆	☐ BELAY DEVICE	☐ HELMET
		☐ QUICKDRAW	☐ HARNESS

CLIMB PARTNER(S)

MILESTONES ACHIEVED	AIMS FOR NEXT CLIMB

ROUTE TAKEN	BETA NOTES

FURTHER OBSERVATIONS

LOCATION		DATE	
CLIMB TYPE			
CLIMB HEIGHT		/ /	

TEMPERATURE		DIFFICULTY RATING	1 2 3 4 5
HUMIDITY			
WEATHER CONDITION	☀ ☁ ❄ ⛈ 💨	TIME OF YEAR	🌷 ☀ 🍃 ❄
START TIME	🕐	**CLIMB CHECKLIST**	
END TIME		☐ CLIMB ROPE	☐ CARABINER
TOTAL TIME TO TOP	⬆	☐ BELAY DEVICE	☐ HELMET
		☐ QUICKDRAW	☐ HARNESS

CLIMB PARTNER(S)

MILESTONES ACHIEVED	AIMS FOR NEXT CLIMB

ROUTE TAKEN	BETA NOTES

FURTHER OBSERVATIONS

LOCATION			DATE				
CLIMB TYPE							
CLIMB HEIGHT			/ /				

TEMPERATURE		DIFFICULTY RATING	1	2	3	4	5
HUMIDITY							
WEATHER CONDITION	☀ ☁ ❄ ⛈ 💨	TIME OF YEAR	🌱 ☀ 🍂 ❄				

START TIME	🕐	CLIMB CHECKLIST	
END TIME		☐ CLIMB ROPE	☐ CARABINER
TOTAL TIME TO TOP	⬆	☐ BELAY DEVICE	☐ HELMET
		☐ QUICKDRAW	☐ HARNESS

CLIMB PARTNER(S)

MILESTONES ACHIEVED	AIMS FOR NEXT CLIMB

ROUTE TAKEN	BETA NOTES

FURTHER OBSERVATIONS

LOCATION		DATE				
CLIMB TYPE						
CLIMB HEIGHT		/ /				

TEMPERATURE		DIFFICULTY RATING	1	2	3	4	5
HUMIDITY							

WEATHER CONDITION	☀ ☁ ❄ ⛈ 💨	TIME OF YEAR	🌷 ☀ 🍃 ❄

START TIME	🕐	CLIMB CHECKLIST	
END TIME		☐ CLIMB ROPE	☐ CARABINER
TOTAL TIME TO TOP	⬆	☐ BELAY DEVICE	☐ HELMET
		☐ QUICKDRAW	☐ HARNESS

CLIMB PARTNER(S)

MILESTONES ACHIEVED | AIMS FOR NEXT CLIMB

ROUTE TAKEN | BETA NOTES

FURTHER OBSERVATIONS

LOCATION		DATE				
CLIMB TYPE						
CLIMB HEIGHT		/ /				

TEMPERATURE		DIFFICULTY RATING	1	2	3	4	5
HUMIDITY							

WEATHER CONDITION	☀ ☁ ❄ ⚡ 〰	TIME OF YEAR	🌷 ☀ 🍃 ❄

START TIME	🕐	CLIMB CHECKLIST	
END TIME		☐ CLIMB ROPE	☐ CARABINER
TOTAL TIME TO TOP	⬆	☐ BELAY DEVICE	☐ HELMET
		☐ QUICKDRAW	☐ HARNESS

CLIMB PARTNER(S)

MILESTONES ACHIEVED	AIMS FOR NEXT CLIMB

ROUTE TAKEN	BETA NOTES

FURTHER OBSERVATIONS

LOCATION		DATE	
CLIMB TYPE			
CLIMB HEIGHT		/ /	

TEMPERATURE		DIFFICULTY RATING	1 2 3 4 5
HUMIDITY			

WEATHER CONDITION	☀ ☁ ❄ ⛈ 🌬	TIME OF YEAR	🌷 ☀ 🍃 ❄

START TIME	🕐	CLIMB CHECKLIST	
END TIME		☐ CLIMB ROPE	☐ CARABINER
TOTAL TIME TO TOP	⬆	☐ BELAY DEVICE	☐ HELMET
		☐ QUICKDRAW	☐ HARNESS

CLIMB PARTNER(S)

MILESTONES ACHIEVED	AIMS FOR NEXT CLIMB

ROUTE TAKEN	BETA NOTES

FURTHER OBSERVATIONS

_____
_____
_____

LOCATION		DATE			
CLIMB TYPE					
CLIMB HEIGHT		/ /			

TEMPERATURE		DIFFICULTY RATING	1	2	3	4	5
HUMIDITY							
WEATHER CONDITION	☀ ☁ ❄ ⛈ 💨	TIME OF YEAR	🌷 ☀ 🍁 ❄				

START TIME	🕐	CLIMB CHECKLIST	
END TIME		☐ CLIMB ROPE	☐ CARABINER
TOTAL TIME TO TOP	⬆	☐ BELAY DEVICE	☐ HELMET
		☐ QUICKDRAW	☐ HARNESS

CLIMB PARTNER(S)

MILESTONES ACHIEVED	AIMS FOR NEXT CLIMB

ROUTE TAKEN	BETA NOTES

FURTHER OBSERVATIONS

LOCATION		DATE				
CLIMB TYPE		/ /				
CLIMB HEIGHT						
TEMPERATURE		DIFFICULTY RATING	1	2	3	4	5
HUMIDITY						

WEATHER CONDITION	☀ ☂ ❄ ⛈ 〰	TIME OF YEAR	🌷 ☀ 🍃 ❄

START TIME	🕐	CLIMB CHECKLIST	
END TIME		☐ CLIMB ROPE	☐ CARABINER
TOTAL TIME TO TOP	⬆	☐ BELAY DEVICE	☐ HELMET
		☐ QUICKDRAW	☐ HARNESS

CLIMB PARTNER(S)

MILESTONES ACHIEVED	AIMS FOR NEXT CLIMB

ROUTE TAKEN	BETA NOTES

FURTHER OBSERVATIONS

LOCATION			DATE	
CLIMB TYPE				
CLIMB HEIGHT				

TEMPERATURE		DIFFICULTY RATING	1 2 3 4 5
HUMIDITY			
WEATHER CONDITION	☀ ☁ ❄ ⛈ 🌬	TIME OF YEAR	🌷 ☀ 🍃 ❄

START TIME	🕐	CLIMB CHECKLIST	
END TIME		☐ CLIMB ROPE	☐ CARABINER
TOTAL TIME TO TOP	⬆	☐ BELAY DEVICE	☐ HELMET
		☐ QUICKDRAW	☐ HARNESS

CLIMB PARTNER(S)

MILESTONES ACHIEVED | AIMS FOR NEXT CLIMB

ROUTE TAKEN | BETA NOTES

FURTHER OBSERVATIONS

LOCATION		DATE				
CLIMB TYPE		/ /				
CLIMB HEIGHT						
TEMPERATURE		DIFFICULTY RATING	1	2	3	4	5
HUMIDITY							
WEATHER CONDITION	☀ ☁ ❄ ⛈ 💨	TIME OF YEAR	🌷 ☀ 🍃 ❄			
START TIME	🕐	**CLIMB CHECKLIST**				
END TIME		☐ CLIMB ROPE	☐ CARABINER			
TOTAL TIME TO TOP	⬆	☐ BELAY DEVICE	☐ HELMET			
		☐ QUICKDRAW	☐ HARNESS			

CLIMB PARTNER(S)

MILESTONES ACHIEVED	AIMS FOR NEXT CLIMB

ROUTE TAKEN	BETA NOTES

FURTHER OBSERVATIONS

___
___
___

LOCATION		DATE		
CLIMB TYPE				
CLIMB HEIGHT		/ /		

TEMPERATURE		DIFFICULTY RATING	1	2	3	4	5
HUMIDITY							

WEATHER CONDITION	☀ ☁ ❄ ⛈ 💨	TIME OF YEAR	🌷 ☀ 🍃 ❄

START TIME	🕐	CLIMB CHECKLIST	
END TIME		☐ CLIMB ROPE	☐ CARABINER
TOTAL TIME TO TOP	⬆	☐ BELAY DEVICE	☐ HELMET
		☐ QUICKDRAW	☐ HARNESS

CLIMB PARTNER(S)

MILESTONES ACHIEVED	AIMS FOR NEXT CLIMB

ROUTE TAKEN	BETA NOTES

FURTHER OBSERVATIONS

LOCATION		DATE	
CLIMB TYPE			
CLIMB HEIGHT		/ /	

TEMPERATURE		DIFFICULTY RATING	1 2 3 4 5
HUMIDITY			

WEATHER CONDITION	☀ ☁ ❄ ⛈ 💨	TIME OF YEAR	🌷 ☀ 🍃 ❄

START TIME	🕐	**CLIMB CHECKLIST**	
END TIME		☐ CLIMB ROPE	☐ CARABINER
TOTAL TIME TO TOP	⬆	☐ BELAY DEVICE	☐ HELMET
		☐ QUICKDRAW	☐ HARNESS

CLIMB PARTNER(S)

MILESTONES ACHIEVED	AIMS FOR NEXT CLIMB

ROUTE TAKEN	BETA NOTES

FURTHER OBSERVATIONS

LOCATION		DATE	
CLIMB TYPE			
CLIMB HEIGHT		/ /	

TEMPERATURE		DIFFICULTY RATING	1 2 3 4 5
HUMIDITY			
WEATHER CONDITION	☀️ 🌧️ ❄️ ⛈️ 💨	TIME OF YEAR	🌷 ☀️ 🍃 ❄️
START TIME	🕐	**CLIMB CHECKLIST**	
END TIME		☐ CLIMB ROPE ☐ CARABINER	
TOTAL TIME TO TOP	⬆	☐ BELAY DEVICE ☐ HELMET	
		☐ QUICKDRAW ☐ HARNESS	

CLIMB PARTNER(S)

MILESTONES ACHIEVED	AIMS FOR NEXT CLIMB

ROUTE TAKEN	BETA NOTES

FURTHER OBSERVATIONS

_____
_____

LOCATION		DATE	
CLIMB TYPE			
CLIMB HEIGHT		/ /	

TEMPERATURE		DIFFICULTY RATING	1	2	3	4	5
HUMIDITY							
WEATHER CONDITION	☀ ☔ ❄ ⛈ 💨	TIME OF YEAR	🌷	☀	🍃	❄	
START TIME	🕐	**CLIMB CHECKLIST**					
END TIME		☐ CLIMB ROPE	☐ CARABINER				
TOTAL TIME TO TOP	⬆	☐ BELAY DEVICE	☐ HELMET				
		☐ QUICKDRAW	☐ HARNESS				

CLIMB PARTNER(S)

MILESTONES ACHIEVED	AIMS FOR NEXT CLIMB

ROUTE TAKEN	BETA NOTES

FURTHER OBSERVATIONS

LOCATION		DATE	
CLIMB TYPE			
CLIMB HEIGHT			

TEMPERATURE		DIFFICULTY RATING	1 2 3 4 5
HUMIDITY			
WEATHER CONDITION	☀ ☁ ❄ ⛈ 〰	TIME OF YEAR	🌷 ☀ 🍁 ❄

START TIME	🕐	CLIMB CHECKLIST	
END TIME		☐ CLIMB ROPE	☐ CARABINER
TOTAL TIME TO TOP	⬆	☐ BELAY DEVICE	☐ HELMET
		☐ QUICKDRAW	☐ HARNESS

CLIMB PARTNER(S)

MILESTONES ACHIEVED	AIMS FOR NEXT CLIMB

ROUTE TAKEN	BETA NOTES

FURTHER OBSERVATIONS

LOCATION		DATE		
CLIMB TYPE				
CLIMB HEIGHT		/ /		

TEMPERATURE		DIFFICULTY RATING	1	2	3	4	5
HUMIDITY							

WEATHER CONDITION		TIME OF YEAR	

START TIME		CLIMB CHECKLIST	
END TIME		☐ CLIMB ROPE	☐ CARABINER
TOTAL TIME TO TOP		☐ BELAY DEVICE	☐ HELMET
		☐ QUICKDRAW	☐ HARNESS

CLIMB PARTNER(S)

MILESTONES ACHIEVED	AIMS FOR NEXT CLIMB

ROUTE TAKEN	BETA NOTES

FURTHER OBSERVATIONS

LOCATION		DATE	
CLIMB TYPE			
CLIMB HEIGHT		/ /	

TEMPERATURE		DIFFICULTY RATING	1 2 3 4 5
HUMIDITY			

WEATHER CONDITION	☀ ☁ ❄ ⛈ 💨	TIME OF YEAR	🌷 ☀ 🍃 ❄

START TIME	🕐	CLIMB CHECKLIST	
END TIME		☐ CLIMB ROPE	☐ CARABINER
TOTAL TIME TO TOP	⬆	☐ BELAY DEVICE	☐ HELMET
		☐ QUICKDRAW	☐ HARNESS

CLIMB PARTNER(S)

MILESTONES ACHIEVED | AIMS FOR NEXT CLIMB

ROUTE TAKEN | BETA NOTES

FURTHER OBSERVATIONS

_____
_____
_____

LOCATION		DATE		
CLIMB TYPE				
CLIMB HEIGHT		/ /		

TEMPERATURE		DIFFICULTY RATING	1 2 3 4 5
HUMIDITY			
WEATHER CONDITION	☀ ☔ ❄ ⛈ 〰	TIME OF YEAR	🌷 ☀ 🍃 ❄

START TIME	🕒	**CLIMB CHECKLIST**	
END TIME		☐ CLIMB ROPE	☐ CARABINER
TOTAL TIME TO TOP	⬆	☐ BELAY DEVICE	☐ HELMET
		☐ QUICKDRAW	☐ HARNESS

CLIMB PARTNER(S)

MILESTONES ACHIEVED | AIMS FOR NEXT CLIMB

ROUTE TAKEN | BETA NOTES

FURTHER OBSERVATIONS

_____
_____
_____

LOCATION		DATE		
CLIMB TYPE		/ /		
CLIMB HEIGHT				

TEMPERATURE		DIFFICULTY RATING	1 2 3 4 5
HUMIDITY			

WEATHER CONDITION	☀ ☁ ❄ ⛈ 🌬	TIME OF YEAR	🌷 ☀ 🍃 ❄

START TIME	🕐	CLIMB CHECKLIST	
END TIME		☐ CLIMB ROPE	☐ CARABINER
TOTAL TIME TO TOP	⬆	☐ BELAY DEVICE	☐ HELMET
		☐ QUICKDRAW	☐ HARNESS

CLIMB PARTNER(S)

MILESTONES ACHIEVED	AIMS FOR NEXT CLIMB

ROUTE TAKEN	BETA NOTES

FURTHER OBSERVATIONS

LOCATION		DATE		
CLIMB TYPE				
CLIMB HEIGHT		/	/	

TEMPERATURE		DIFFICULTY RATING	1	2	3	4	5
HUMIDITY							
WEATHER CONDITION	☀ ☁ ❄ ⛈ 🌬	TIME OF YEAR	🌷 ☀ 🍃 ❄				
START TIME	🕐	CLIMB CHECKLIST					
END TIME		☐ CLIMB ROPE ☐ CARABINER					
TOTAL TIME TO TOP	⬆	☐ BELAY DEVICE ☐ HELMET					
		☐ QUICKDRAW ☐ HARNESS					

CLIMB PARTNER(S)

MILESTONES ACHIEVED	AIMS FOR NEXT CLIMB

ROUTE TAKEN	BETA NOTES

FURTHER OBSERVATIONS

LOCATION		DATE				
CLIMB TYPE						
CLIMB HEIGHT		/ /				

TEMPERATURE		DIFFICULTY RATING	1	2	3	4	5
HUMIDITY							

WEATHER CONDITION	☀ ☁ ❄ ⛈ 〰	TIME OF YEAR	🌷 ☀ 🍃 ❄

START TIME	🕐	CLIMB CHECKLIST	
END TIME		☐ CLIMB ROPE	☐ CARABINER
TOTAL TIME TO TOP	⬆	☐ BELAY DEVICE	☐ HELMET
		☐ QUICKDRAW	☐ HARNESS

CLIMB PARTNER(S)

MILESTONES ACHIEVED	AIMS FOR NEXT CLIMB

ROUTE TAKEN	BETA NOTES

FURTHER OBSERVATIONS

LOCATION		DATE				
CLIMB TYPE						
CLIMB HEIGHT		/ /				

TEMPERATURE		DIFFICULTY RATING	1	2	3	4	5
HUMIDITY							

WEATHER CONDITION	☀ ☁ ❄ ⛈ 🌬	TIME OF YEAR	🌷 ☀ 🍃 ❄

START TIME	🕐	CLIMB CHECKLIST	
END TIME		☐ CLIMB ROPE	☐ CARABINER
TOTAL TIME TO TOP	⬆	☐ BELAY DEVICE	☐ HELMET
		☐ QUICKDRAW	☐ HARNESS

CLIMB PARTNER(S)

MILESTONES ACHIEVED	AIMS FOR NEXT CLIMB

ROUTE TAKEN	BETA NOTES

FURTHER OBSERVATIONS

LOCATION		DATE	
CLIMB TYPE			
CLIMB HEIGHT		/ /	

TEMPERATURE		DIFFICULTY RATING	1 2 3 4 5
HUMIDITY			

WEATHER CONDITION	☀ ☁ ❄ ⛈ 💨	TIME OF YEAR	🌷 ☀ 🍃 ❄

START TIME	🕐	CLIMB CHECKLIST	
END TIME		☐ CLIMB ROPE	☐ CARABINER
TOTAL TIME TO TOP	⬆	☐ BELAY DEVICE	☐ HELMET
		☐ QUICKDRAW	☐ HARNESS

CLIMB PARTNER(S)

MILESTONES ACHIEVED	AIMS FOR NEXT CLIMB

ROUTE TAKEN	BETA NOTES

FURTHER OBSERVATIONS

LOCATION		DATE			
CLIMB TYPE					
CLIMB HEIGHT		/ /			

TEMPERATURE		DIFFICULTY RATING	1	2	3	4	5
HUMIDITY							
WEATHER CONDITION	☀ ☁ ❄ ⛈ 💨	TIME OF YEAR	🌷 ☀ 🍃 ❄				

START TIME	🕐	CLIMB CHECKLIST	
END TIME		☐ CLIMB ROPE	☐ CARABINER
TOTAL TIME TO TOP	⬆	☐ BELAY DEVICE	☐ HELMET
		☐ QUICKDRAW	☐ HARNESS

CLIMB PARTNER(S)

MILESTONES ACHIEVED	AIMS FOR NEXT CLIMB

ROUTE TAKEN	BETA NOTES

FURTHER OBSERVATIONS

_____
_____
_____

LOCATION		DATE	
CLIMB TYPE			
CLIMB HEIGHT		/ /	

TEMPERATURE		DIFFICULTY RATING	1 2 3 4 5
HUMIDITY			
WEATHER CONDITION	☀ ☂ ❄ ⛈ 〰	TIME OF YEAR	🌷 ☀ 🍃 ❄

START TIME	🕐	**CLIMB CHECKLIST**	
END TIME		☐ CLIMB ROPE	☐ CARABINER
TOTAL TIME TO TOP	⬆	☐ BELAY DEVICE	☐ HELMET
		☐ QUICKDRAW	☐ HARNESS

CLIMB PARTNER(S)

MILESTONES ACHIEVED	AIMS FOR NEXT CLIMB

ROUTE TAKEN	BETA NOTES

FURTHER OBSERVATIONS

_____
_____
_____

LOCATION		DATE				
CLIMB TYPE						
CLIMB HEIGHT		/ /				

TEMPERATURE		DIFFICULTY RATING	1	2	3	4	5
HUMIDITY							

WEATHER CONDITION	☀ ☁ ❄ ⛈ 🌬	TIME OF YEAR	🌷 ☀ 🍃 ❄

START TIME	🕐	CLIMB CHECKLIST			
END TIME		☐ CLIMB ROPE	☐ CARABINER		
TOTAL TIME TO TOP	⬆	☐ BELAY DEVICE	☐ HELMET		
		☐ QUICKDRAW	☐ HARNESS		

CLIMB PARTNER(S)

MILESTONES ACHIEVED	AIMS FOR NEXT CLIMB

ROUTE TAKEN	BETA NOTES

FURTHER OBSERVATIONS

LOCATION			DATE			
CLIMB TYPE						
CLIMB HEIGHT						

TEMPERATURE		DIFFICULTY RATING	1	2	3	4	5
HUMIDITY							
WEATHER CONDITION	☀ ☁ ❄ ⛈ 💨	TIME OF YEAR	🌷 ☀ 🍁 ❄				
START TIME	🕐	**CLIMB CHECKLIST**					
END TIME		☐ CLIMB ROPE ☐ CARABINER					
TOTAL TIME TO TOP	⬆	☐ BELAY DEVICE ☐ HELMET					
		☐ QUICKDRAW ☐ HARNESS					

CLIMB PARTNER(S)

MILESTONES ACHIEVED	AIMS FOR NEXT CLIMB

ROUTE TAKEN	BETA NOTES

FURTHER OBSERVATIONS

LOCATION		DATE	
CLIMB TYPE			
CLIMB HEIGHT		/ /	

TEMPERATURE		DIFFICULTY RATING	1 2 3 4 5
HUMIDITY			
WEATHER CONDITION	☀ ☁ ❄ ⛈ 💨	TIME OF YEAR	🌷 ☀ 🍃 ❄

START TIME	🕐	CLIMB CHECKLIST	
END TIME		☐ CLIMB ROPE	☐ CARABINER
TOTAL TIME TO TOP	⬆	☐ BELAY DEVICE	☐ HELMET
		☐ QUICKDRAW	☐ HARNESS

CLIMB PARTNER(S)

MILESTONES ACHIEVED	AIMS FOR NEXT CLIMB

ROUTE TAKEN	BETA NOTES

FURTHER OBSERVATIONS

LOCATION		DATE			
CLIMB TYPE		/ /			
CLIMB HEIGHT					

TEMPERATURE		DIFFICULTY RATING	1	2	3	4	5
HUMIDITY							

WEATHER CONDITION	☀ ☁ ❄ ⛈ 💨	TIME OF YEAR	🌷 ☀ 🍂 ❄

START TIME	🕐	CLIMB CHECKLIST	
END TIME		☐ CLIMB ROPE	☐ CARABINER
TOTAL TIME TO TOP	⬆	☐ BELAY DEVICE	☐ HELMET
		☐ QUICKDRAW	☐ HARNESS

CLIMB PARTNER(S)

MILESTONES ACHIEVED | AIMS FOR NEXT CLIMB

ROUTE TAKEN | BETA NOTES

FURTHER OBSERVATIONS

LOCATION		DATE		
CLIMB TYPE				
CLIMB HEIGHT		/ /		

TEMPERATURE		DIFFICULTY RATING	1 2 3 4 5
HUMIDITY			
WEATHER CONDITION	☀ ☂ ❄ ⛈ 〜	TIME OF YEAR	🌷 ☀ 🍃 ❄

START TIME	🕐	**CLIMB CHECKLIST**	
END TIME		☐ CLIMB ROPE	☐ CARABINER
TOTAL TIME TO TOP	⬆	☐ BELAY DEVICE	☐ HELMET
		☐ QUICKDRAW	☐ HARNESS

CLIMB PARTNER(S)

MILESTONES ACHIEVED	AIMS FOR NEXT CLIMB

ROUTE TAKEN	BETA NOTES

FURTHER OBSERVATIONS

_____
_____
_____

LOCATION		DATE				
CLIMB TYPE						
CLIMB HEIGHT		/ /				

TEMPERATURE		DIFFICULTY RATING	1	2	3	4	5
HUMIDITY							
WEATHER CONDITION	☀ ☁ ❄ ⛈ 💨	TIME OF YEAR	🌷 ☀ 🍃 ❄				

START TIME	🕐	**CLIMB CHECKLIST**	
END TIME		☐ CLIMB ROPE	☐ CARABINER
TOTAL TIME TO TOP	⬆	☐ BELAY DEVICE	☐ HELMET
		☐ QUICKDRAW	☐ HARNESS

CLIMB PARTNER(S)

MILESTONES ACHIEVED	AIMS FOR NEXT CLIMB

ROUTE TAKEN	BETA NOTES

FURTHER OBSERVATIONS

LOCATION			DATE	
CLIMB TYPE				
CLIMB HEIGHT			/ /	

TEMPERATURE		DIFFICULTY RATING	1 2 3 4 5
HUMIDITY			
WEATHER CONDITION	☀ ☁ ❄ ⛈ 🌬	TIME OF YEAR	🌷 ☀ 🍃 ❄
START TIME	🕐	**CLIMB CHECKLIST**	
END TIME		☐ CLIMB ROPE ☐ CARABINER	
TOTAL TIME TO TOP	⬆	☐ BELAY DEVICE ☐ HELMET	
		☐ QUICKDRAW ☐ HARNESS	

CLIMB PARTNER(S)

MILESTONES ACHIEVED	AIMS FOR NEXT CLIMB

ROUTE TAKEN	BETA NOTES

FURTHER OBSERVATIONS

LOCATION		DATE				
CLIMB TYPE		/ /				
CLIMB HEIGHT						

TEMPERATURE		DIFFICULTY RATING	1	2	3	4	5
HUMIDITY							

WEATHER CONDITION	☀ ☁ ❄ ⛈ 💨	TIME OF YEAR	🌱 ☀ 🍃 ❄

START TIME	🕐	CLIMB CHECKLIST	
END TIME		☐ CLIMB ROPE	☐ CARABINER
TOTAL TIME TO TOP	⬆	☐ BELAY DEVICE	☐ HELMET
		☐ QUICKDRAW	☐ HARNESS

CLIMB PARTNER(S)

MILESTONES ACHIEVED	AIMS FOR NEXT CLIMB

ROUTE TAKEN	BETA NOTES

FURTHER OBSERVATIONS

LOCATION		DATE	
CLIMB TYPE			
CLIMB HEIGHT		/ /	

TEMPERATURE		DIFFICULTY RATING	1 2 3 4 5
HUMIDITY			
WEATHER CONDITION	☀ ☁ ❄ ⛈ 💨	TIME OF YEAR	🌷 ☀ 🍃 ❄
START TIME	🕐	**CLIMB CHECKLIST**	
END TIME		☐ CLIMB ROPE	☐ CARABINER
TOTAL TIME TO TOP	⬆	☐ BELAY DEVICE	☐ HELMET
		☐ QUICKDRAW	☐ HARNESS

CLIMB PARTNER(S)

MILESTONES ACHIEVED	AIMS FOR NEXT CLIMB

ROUTE TAKEN	BETA NOTES

FURTHER OBSERVATIONS

LOCATION		DATE				
CLIMB TYPE						
CLIMB HEIGHT		/ /				

TEMPERATURE		DIFFICULTY RATING	1	2	3	4	5
HUMIDITY							

WEATHER CONDITION	☀ ☁ ❄ ⛈ 🌬	TIME OF YEAR	🌷 ☀ 🍃 ❄

START TIME	🕐	CLIMB CHECKLIST	
END TIME		☐ CLIMB ROPE	☐ CARABINER
TOTAL TIME TO TOP	⬆	☐ BELAY DEVICE	☐ HELMET
		☐ QUICKDRAW	☐ HARNESS

CLIMB PARTNER(S)

MILESTONES ACHIEVED | AIMS FOR NEXT CLIMB

ROUTE TAKEN | BETA NOTES

FURTHER OBSERVATIONS

_____
_____
_____

LOCATION		DATE	
CLIMB TYPE			
CLIMB HEIGHT		/ /	

TEMPERATURE		DIFFICULTY RATING	1 2 3 4 5
HUMIDITY			

WEATHER CONDITION	☀ ☁ ❄ ⛈ 💨	TIME OF YEAR	🌷 ☀ 🍃 ❄

START TIME	🕐	CLIMB CHECKLIST	
END TIME		☐ CLIMB ROPE	☐ CARABINER
TOTAL TIME TO TOP	⬆	☐ BELAY DEVICE	☐ HELMET
		☐ QUICKDRAW	☐ HARNESS

CLIMB PARTNER(S)

MILESTONES ACHIEVED	AIMS FOR NEXT CLIMB

ROUTE TAKEN	BETA NOTES

FURTHER OBSERVATIONS

_____
_____
_____

LOCATION		DATE			
CLIMB TYPE		/ /			
CLIMB HEIGHT					

TEMPERATURE		DIFFICULTY RATING	1	2	3	4	5
HUMIDITY							
WEATHER CONDITION	☀ ☁ ❄ ⛈ 〰	TIME OF YEAR	🌷 ☀ 🍃 ❄				

START TIME	🕐	CLIMB CHECKLIST	
END TIME		☐ CLIMB ROPE	☐ CARABINER
TOTAL TIME TO TOP	⬆	☐ BELAY DEVICE	☐ HELMET
		☐ QUICKDRAW	☐ HARNESS

CLIMB PARTNER(S)

MILESTONES ACHIEVED	AIMS FOR NEXT CLIMB

ROUTE TAKEN	BETA NOTES

FURTHER OBSERVATIONS

___
___
___

LOCATION		DATE	
CLIMB TYPE			
CLIMB HEIGHT		/ /	

TEMPERATURE		DIFFICULTY RATING	1 2 3 4 5
HUMIDITY			
WEATHER CONDITION	☀ ☔ ❄ ⛈ 💨	TIME OF YEAR	🌷 ☀ 🍃 ❄
START TIME	🕐	**CLIMB CHECKLIST**	
END TIME		☐ CLIMB ROPE ☐ CARABINER	
TOTAL TIME TO TOP	⬆	☐ BELAY DEVICE ☐ HELMET	
		☐ QUICKDRAW ☐ HARNESS	

CLIMB PARTNER(S)

MILESTONES ACHIEVED	AIMS FOR NEXT CLIMB

ROUTE TAKEN	BETA NOTES

FURTHER OBSERVATIONS

_____

_____

_____

LOCATION		DATE	
CLIMB TYPE			
CLIMB HEIGHT		/ /	

TEMPERATURE		DIFFICULTY RATING	1 2 3 4 5
HUMIDITY			

WEATHER CONDITION	☀ ☁ ❄ ⛈ 🌬	TIME OF YEAR	🌷 ☀ 🍃 ❄

START TIME	🕐	CLIMB CHECKLIST	
END TIME		☐ CLIMB ROPE	☐ CARABINER
TOTAL TIME TO TOP	⬆	☐ BELAY DEVICE	☐ HELMET
		☐ QUICKDRAW	☐ HARNESS

CLIMB PARTNER(S)

MILESTONES ACHIEVED	AIMS FOR NEXT CLIMB

ROUTE TAKEN	BETA NOTES

FURTHER OBSERVATIONS

LOCATION		DATE				
CLIMB TYPE						
CLIMB HEIGHT		/ /				

TEMPERATURE		DIFFICULTY RATING	1	2	3	4	5
HUMIDITY							

WEATHER CONDITION	☀ ☁ ❄ ⛈ 💨	TIME OF YEAR	🌷 ☀ 🍃 ❄

START TIME	🕐	CLIMB CHECKLIST	
END TIME		☐ CLIMB ROPE	☐ CARABINER
TOTAL TIME TO TOP	⬆	☐ BELAY DEVICE	☐ HELMET
		☐ QUICKDRAW	☐ HARNESS

CLIMB PARTNER(S)

MILESTONES ACHIEVED	AIMS FOR NEXT CLIMB

ROUTE TAKEN	BETA NOTES

FURTHER OBSERVATIONS

LOCATION		DATE		
CLIMB TYPE		/ /		
CLIMB HEIGHT				

TEMPERATURE		DIFFICULTY RATING	1 2 3 4 5
HUMIDITY			

WEATHER CONDITION	☀ ☁ ❄ ⛈ 🌬	TIME OF YEAR	🌷 ☀ 🍃 ❄

START TIME	🕐	CLIMB CHECKLIST	
END TIME		☐ CLIMB ROPE	☐ CARABINER
TOTAL TIME TO TOP	⬆	☐ BELAY DEVICE	☐ HELMET
		☐ QUICKDRAW	☐ HARNESS

CLIMB PARTNER(S)

MILESTONES ACHIEVED	AIMS FOR NEXT CLIMB

ROUTE TAKEN	BETA NOTES

FURTHER OBSERVATIONS

LOCATION		DATE		
CLIMB TYPE				
CLIMB HEIGHT		/ /		

TEMPERATURE		DIFFICULTY RATING	1 2 3 4 5
HUMIDITY			

WEATHER CONDITION	☀ 🌧 ❄ ⛈ 🌬	TIME OF YEAR	🌷 ☀ 🍃 ❄

START TIME	🕐	CLIMB CHECKLIST	
END TIME		☐ CLIMB ROPE	☐ CARABINER
TOTAL TIME TO TOP	⬆	☐ BELAY DEVICE	☐ HELMET
		☐ QUICKDRAW	☐ HARNESS

CLIMB PARTNER(S)

MILESTONES ACHIEVED	AIMS FOR NEXT CLIMB

ROUTE TAKEN	BETA NOTES

FURTHER OBSERVATIONS

LOCATION		DATE			
CLIMB TYPE		/ /			
CLIMB HEIGHT					

TEMPERATURE		DIFFICULTY RATING	1	2	3	4	5
HUMIDITY							
WEATHER CONDITION	☀ ☁ ❄ ⛈ 💨	TIME OF YEAR	🌷 ☀ 🍃 ❄				

START TIME	🕐	CLIMB CHECKLIST	
END TIME		☐ CLIMB ROPE	☐ CARABINER
TOTAL TIME TO TOP	⬆	☐ BELAY DEVICE	☐ HELMET
		☐ QUICKDRAW	☐ HARNESS

CLIMB PARTNER(S)

MILESTONES ACHIEVED	AIMS FOR NEXT CLIMB

ROUTE TAKEN	BETA NOTES

FURTHER OBSERVATIONS

LOCATION		DATE				
CLIMB TYPE		/ /				
CLIMB HEIGHT						
TEMPERATURE		DIFFICULTY RATING	1	2	3	4	5
HUMIDITY						
WEATHER CONDITION	☀ ☂ ❄ ⛈ 💨	TIME OF YEAR	🌷 ☀ 🍃 ❄
START TIME	🕐	CLIMB CHECKLIST	
END TIME		☐ CLIMB ROPE	☐ CARABINER
TOTAL TIME TO TOP	⬆	☐ BELAY DEVICE	☐ HELMET
		☐ QUICKDRAW	☐ HARNESS

CLIMB PARTNER(S)

MILESTONES ACHIEVED | AIMS FOR NEXT CLIMB

ROUTE TAKEN | BETA NOTES

FURTHER OBSERVATIONS

LOCATION			DATE				
CLIMB TYPE			/ /				
CLIMB HEIGHT							

TEMPERATURE		DIFFICULTY RATING	1	2	3	4	5
HUMIDITY							

WEATHER CONDITION	☀ ☁ ❄ ⛈ 〰	TIME OF YEAR	🌷 ☀ 🍁 ❄

START TIME	🕐	CLIMB CHECKLIST	
END TIME		☐ CLIMB ROPE	☐ CARABINER
TOTAL TIME TO TOP	⬆	☐ BELAY DEVICE	☐ HELMET
		☐ QUICKDRAW	☐ HARNESS

CLIMB PARTNER(S)

MILESTONES ACHIEVED	AIMS FOR NEXT CLIMB

ROUTE TAKEN	BETA NOTES

FURTHER OBSERVATIONS

LOCATION		DATE	
CLIMB TYPE			
CLIMB HEIGHT		/ /	

TEMPERATURE		DIFFICULTY RATING	1 2 3 4 5
HUMIDITY			
WEATHER CONDITION	☀ ☁ ❄ ⛈ 💨	TIME OF YEAR	🌷 ☀ 🍃 ❄
START TIME	🕐	**CLIMB CHECKLIST**	
END TIME		☐ CLIMB ROPE	☐ CARABINER
TOTAL TIME TO TOP	⬆	☐ BELAY DEVICE	☐ HELMET
		☐ QUICKDRAW	☐ HARNESS

CLIMB PARTNER(S)

MILESTONES ACHIEVED	AIMS FOR NEXT CLIMB

ROUTE TAKEN	BETA NOTES

FURTHER OBSERVATIONS

_____
_____
_____

LOCATION		DATE				
CLIMB TYPE						
CLIMB HEIGHT		/ /				

TEMPERATURE		DIFFICULTY RATING	1	2	3	4	5
HUMIDITY							

WEATHER CONDITION	☀ ☁ ❄ ⛈ 💨	TIME OF YEAR	🌷 ☀ 🍃 ❄

START TIME	🕐	CLIMB CHECKLIST	
END TIME		☐ CLIMB ROPE	☐ CARABINER
TOTAL TIME TO TOP	⬆	☐ BELAY DEVICE	☐ HELMET
		☐ QUICKDRAW	☐ HARNESS

CLIMB PARTNER(S)

MILESTONES ACHIEVED	AIMS FOR NEXT CLIMB

ROUTE TAKEN	BETA NOTES

FURTHER OBSERVATIONS

LOCATION		DATE	
CLIMB TYPE			
CLIMB HEIGHT		/ /	

TEMPERATURE		DIFFICULTY RATING	1 2 3 4 5
HUMIDITY			
WEATHER CONDITION	☀ ☔ ❄ ⛈ 〰	TIME OF YEAR	🌷 ☀ 🍃 ❄
START TIME	🕐	**CLIMB CHECKLIST**	
END TIME		☐ CLIMB ROPE ☐ CARABINER	
TOTAL TIME TO TOP	⬆	☐ BELAY DEVICE ☐ HELMET	
		☐ QUICKDRAW ☐ HARNESS	

CLIMB PARTNER(S)

MILESTONES ACHIEVED	AIMS FOR NEXT CLIMB

ROUTE TAKEN	BETA NOTES

FURTHER OBSERVATIONS

___
___
___

LOCATION		DATE	
CLIMB TYPE			
CLIMB HEIGHT		/ /	

TEMPERATURE		DIFFICULTY RATING	1 2 3 4 5
HUMIDITY			
WEATHER CONDITION	☀ ☁ ❄ ⚡ 💨	TIME OF YEAR	🌷 ☀ 🍁 ❄

START TIME	🕐	CLIMB CHECKLIST	
END TIME		☐ CLIMB ROPE	☐ CARABINER
TOTAL TIME TO TOP	⬆	☐ BELAY DEVICE	☐ HELMET
		☐ QUICKDRAW	☐ HARNESS

CLIMB PARTNER(S)

MILESTONES ACHIEVED | AIMS FOR NEXT CLIMB

ROUTE TAKEN | BETA NOTES

FURTHER OBSERVATIONS

LOCATION		DATE
CLIMB TYPE		
CLIMB HEIGHT		/ /

TEMPERATURE		DIFFICULTY RATING	1	2	3	4	5
HUMIDITY							

WEATHER CONDITION		TIME OF YEAR	

START TIME		CLIMB CHECKLIST	
END TIME		☐ CLIMB ROPE	☐ CARABINER
TOTAL TIME TO TOP		☐ BELAY DEVICE	☐ HELMET
		☐ QUICKDRAW	☐ HARNESS

CLIMB PARTNER(S)

MILESTONES ACHIEVED	AIMS FOR NEXT CLIMB

ROUTE TAKEN	BETA NOTES

FURTHER OBSERVATIONS

LOCATION		DATE	
CLIMB TYPE			
CLIMB HEIGHT		/ /	

TEMPERATURE		DIFFICULTY RATING	1 2 3 4 5
HUMIDITY			
WEATHER CONDITION	☀ ☁ ❄ ⛈ 🌬	TIME OF YEAR	🌷 ☀ 🍁 ❄

START TIME	🕐	CLIMB CHECKLIST	
END TIME		☐ CLIMB ROPE	☐ CARABINER
TOTAL TIME TO TOP	⬆	☐ BELAY DEVICE	☐ HELMET
		☐ QUICKDRAW	☐ HARNESS

CLIMB PARTNER(S)

MILESTONES ACHIEVED	AIMS FOR NEXT CLIMB

ROUTE TAKEN	BETA NOTES

FURTHER OBSERVATIONS

LOCATION		DATE		
CLIMB TYPE				
CLIMB HEIGHT		/ /		

TEMPERATURE		DIFFICULTY RATING	1	2	3	4	5
HUMIDITY							

WEATHER CONDITION	☀ ☁ ❄ ⛈ 〰	TIME OF YEAR	🌷 ☀ 🍁 ❄

START TIME	🕐	CLIMB CHECKLIST	
END TIME		☐ CLIMB ROPE	☐ CARABINER
TOTAL TIME TO TOP	⬆	☐ BELAY DEVICE	☐ HELMET
		☐ QUICKDRAW	☐ HARNESS

CLIMB PARTNER(S)

MILESTONES ACHIEVED	AIMS FOR NEXT CLIMB

ROUTE TAKEN	BETA NOTES

FURTHER OBSERVATIONS

___
___
___

LOCATION		DATE	
CLIMB TYPE			
CLIMB HEIGHT		/ /	

TEMPERATURE		DIFFICULTY RATING	1 2 3 4 5
HUMIDITY			

WEATHER CONDITION	☀ ☁ ❄ ⚡ 💨	TIME OF YEAR	🌷 ☀ 🍃 ❄

START TIME	🕐	**CLIMB CHECKLIST**	
END TIME		☐ CLIMB ROPE	☐ CARABINER
TOTAL TIME TO TOP	⬆	☐ BELAY DEVICE	☐ HELMET
		☐ QUICKDRAW	☐ HARNESS

CLIMB PARTNER(S)

MILESTONES ACHIEVED	AIMS FOR NEXT CLIMB

ROUTE TAKEN	BETA NOTES

FURTHER OBSERVATIONS

LOCATION		DATE	
CLIMB TYPE			
CLIMB HEIGHT		/ /	

TEMPERATURE		DIFFICULTY RATING	1 2 3 4 5
HUMIDITY			

WEATHER CONDITION	☀ ☔ ❄ ⛈ 〰	TIME OF YEAR	🌷 ☀ 🍃 ❄

START TIME	🕐	CLIMB CHECKLIST	
END TIME		☐ CLIMB ROPE	☐ CARABINER
TOTAL TIME TO TOP	⬆	☐ BELAY DEVICE	☐ HELMET
		☐ QUICKDRAW	☐ HARNESS

CLIMB PARTNER(S)

MILESTONES ACHIEVED | AIMS FOR NEXT CLIMB

ROUTE TAKEN | BETA NOTES

FURTHER OBSERVATIONS

_____
_____
_____

LOCATION		DATE			
CLIMB TYPE					
CLIMB HEIGHT		/ /			

TEMPERATURE		DIFFICULTY RATING	1	2	3	4	5
HUMIDITY							
WEATHER CONDITION	☀️ 🌧️ ❄️ ⛈️ 💨	TIME OF YEAR	🌷 ☀️ 🍃 ❄️				

START TIME	🕐	CLIMB CHECKLIST	
END TIME		☐ CLIMB ROPE	☐ CARABINER
TOTAL TIME TO TOP	⬆️	☐ BELAY DEVICE	☐ HELMET
		☐ QUICKDRAW	☐ HARNESS

CLIMB PARTNER(S)

MILESTONES ACHIEVED	AIMS FOR NEXT CLIMB

ROUTE TAKEN	BETA NOTES

FURTHER OBSERVATIONS

LOCATION		DATE		
CLIMB TYPE		/ /		
CLIMB HEIGHT				

TEMPERATURE		DIFFICULTY RATING	1	2	3	4	5
HUMIDITY							
WEATHER CONDITION	☀ ☂ ❄ ⛈ 〰	TIME OF YEAR	🌷	☀	🍃	❄	
START TIME	🕐	**CLIMB CHECKLIST**					
END TIME		☐ CLIMB ROPE		☐ CARABINER			
TOTAL TIME TO TOP	⬆	☐ BELAY DEVICE		☐ HELMET			
		☐ QUICKDRAW		☐ HARNESS			

CLIMB PARTNER(S)

MILESTONES ACHIEVED	AIMS FOR NEXT CLIMB

ROUTE TAKEN	BETA NOTES

FURTHER OBSERVATIONS

LOCATION		DATE				
CLIMB TYPE						
CLIMB HEIGHT		/ /				

TEMPERATURE		DIFFICULTY RATING	1	2	3	4	5
HUMIDITY							

WEATHER CONDITION	☀ ☁ ❄ ⛈ 🌬	TIME OF YEAR	🌸 ☀ 🍃 ❄

START TIME	🕐	CLIMB CHECKLIST	
END TIME		☐ CLIMB ROPE	☐ CARABINER
TOTAL TIME TO TOP	⬆	☐ BELAY DEVICE	☐ HELMET
		☐ QUICKDRAW	☐ HARNESS

CLIMB PARTNER(S)

MILESTONES ACHIEVED	AIMS FOR NEXT CLIMB

ROUTE TAKEN	BETA NOTES

FURTHER OBSERVATIONS

LOCATION		DATE				
CLIMB TYPE						
CLIMB HEIGHT		/ /				

TEMPERATURE		DIFFICULTY RATING	1	2	3	4	5
HUMIDITY							

WEATHER CONDITION	☀ ☁ ❄ ⛈ 🌬	TIME OF YEAR	🌷 ☀ 🍃 ❄

START TIME	🕐	CLIMB CHECKLIST	
END TIME		☐ CLIMB ROPE	☐ CARABINER
TOTAL TIME TO TOP	⬆	☐ BELAY DEVICE	☐ HELMET
		☐ QUICKDRAW	☐ HARNESS

CLIMB PARTNER(S)

MILESTONES ACHIEVED	AIMS FOR NEXT CLIMB

ROUTE TAKEN	BETA NOTES

FURTHER OBSERVATIONS

_____
_____
_____

LOCATION		DATE				
CLIMB TYPE						
CLIMB HEIGHT		/ /				

TEMPERATURE		DIFFICULTY RATING	1	2	3	4	5
HUMIDITY							

WEATHER CONDITION	☀ ☁ ❄ ⛈ 🌬	TIME OF YEAR	🌷 ☀ 🍃 ❄

START TIME	🕐	CLIMB CHECKLIST	
END TIME		☐ CLIMB ROPE	☐ CARABINER
TOTAL TIME TO TOP	⬆	☐ BELAY DEVICE	☐ HELMET
		☐ QUICKDRAW	☐ HARNESS

CLIMB PARTNER(S)

MILESTONES ACHIEVED | AIMS FOR NEXT CLIMB

ROUTE TAKEN | BETA NOTES

FURTHER OBSERVATIONS

_____
_____
_____

LOCATION		DATE	
CLIMB TYPE			
CLIMB HEIGHT		/ /	

TEMPERATURE		DIFFICULTY RATING	1 2 3 4 5
HUMIDITY			

WEATHER CONDITION	☀ ☂ ❄ ⚡ 〰	TIME OF YEAR	🌷 ☀ 🍃 ❄

START TIME	🕐	CLIMB CHECKLIST	
END TIME		☐ CLIMB ROPE	☐ CARABINER
TOTAL TIME TO TOP	⬆	☐ BELAY DEVICE	☐ HELMET
		☐ QUICKDRAW	☐ HARNESS

CLIMB PARTNER(S)

MILESTONES ACHIEVED	AIMS FOR NEXT CLIMB

ROUTE TAKEN	BETA NOTES

FURTHER OBSERVATIONS

_____
_____
_____

LOCATION		DATE	
CLIMB TYPE			
CLIMB HEIGHT		/ /	

TEMPERATURE		DIFFICULTY RATING	1 2 3 4 5
HUMIDITY			
WEATHER CONDITION	☀ ☁ ❄ ⛈ 💨	TIME OF YEAR	🌷 ☀ 🍃 ❄

START TIME		CLIMB CHECKLIST	
END TIME		☐ CLIMB ROPE	☐ CARABINER
TOTAL TIME TO TOP	⬆	☐ BELAY DEVICE	☐ HELMET
		☐ QUICKDRAW	☐ HARNESS

CLIMB PARTNER(S)

MILESTONES ACHIEVED | AIMS FOR NEXT CLIMB

ROUTE TAKEN | BETA NOTES

FURTHER OBSERVATIONS

_____
_____

LOCATION		DATE		
CLIMB TYPE				
CLIMB HEIGHT		/ /		

TEMPERATURE		DIFFICULTY RATING	1	2	3	4	5
HUMIDITY							

WEATHER CONDITION	☀ ☁ ❄ ⛈ 💨	TIME OF YEAR	🌷 ☀ 🍃 ❄

START TIME	🕐	CLIMB CHECKLIST	
END TIME		☐ CLIMB ROPE	☐ CARABINER
TOTAL TIME TO TOP	⬆	☐ BELAY DEVICE	☐ HELMET
		☐ QUICKDRAW	☐ HARNESS

CLIMB PARTNER(S)

MILESTONES ACHIEVED	AIMS FOR NEXT CLIMB

ROUTE TAKEN	BETA NOTES

FURTHER OBSERVATIONS

LOCATION		DATE	
CLIMB TYPE			
CLIMB HEIGHT		/ /	

TEMPERATURE		DIFFICULTY RATING	1 2 3 4 5
HUMIDITY			
WEATHER CONDITION	☀ ☁ ❄ ⛈ 〰	TIME OF YEAR	🌷 ☀ 🍃 ❄

START TIME	🕐	**CLIMB CHECKLIST**	
END TIME		☐ CLIMB ROPE	☐ CARABINER
TOTAL TIME TO TOP	⬆	☐ BELAY DEVICE	☐ HELMET
		☐ QUICKDRAW	☐ HARNESS

CLIMB PARTNER(S)

MILESTONES ACHIEVED	AIMS FOR NEXT CLIMB

ROUTE TAKEN	BETA NOTES

FURTHER OBSERVATIONS

___
___
___

LOCATION		DATE		
CLIMB TYPE				
CLIMB HEIGHT		/ /		

TEMPERATURE		DIFFICULTY RATING	1	2	3	4	5
HUMIDITY							

WEATHER CONDITION	☀ ☁ ❄ ⛈ 💨	TIME OF YEAR	🌷 ☀ 🍃 ❄

START TIME	🕐	CLIMB CHECKLIST	
END TIME		☐ CLIMB ROPE	☐ CARABINER
TOTAL TIME TO TOP	⬆	☐ BELAY DEVICE	☐ HELMET
		☐ QUICKDRAW	☐ HARNESS

CLIMB PARTNER(S)

MILESTONES ACHIEVED	AIMS FOR NEXT CLIMB

ROUTE TAKEN	BETA NOTES

FURTHER OBSERVATIONS

___
___
___

LOCATION		DATE
CLIMB TYPE		
CLIMB HEIGHT		/ /

TEMPERATURE		DIFFICULTY RATING	1 2 3 4 5
HUMIDITY			
WEATHER CONDITION	☀ ☁ ❄ ⛈ 🌬	TIME OF YEAR	🌷 ☀ 🍃 ❄

START TIME	🕐	CLIMB CHECKLIST	
END TIME		☐ CLIMB ROPE	☐ CARABINER
TOTAL TIME TO TOP	⬆	☐ BELAY DEVICE	☐ HELMET
		☐ QUICKDRAW	☐ HARNESS

CLIMB PARTNER(S)

MILESTONES ACHIEVED	AIMS FOR NEXT CLIMB

ROUTE TAKEN	BETA NOTES

FURTHER OBSERVATIONS

LOCATION		DATE	
CLIMB TYPE			
CLIMB HEIGHT		/ /	

TEMPERATURE		DIFFICULTY RATING	1 2 3 4 5
HUMIDITY			

WEATHER CONDITION	☀ ☂ ❄ ⛈ 💨	TIME OF YEAR	🌷 ☀ 🍃 ❄

START TIME	🕐	CLIMB CHECKLIST	
END TIME		☐ CLIMB ROPE	☐ CARABINER
TOTAL TIME TO TOP	⬆	☐ BELAY DEVICE	☐ HELMET
		☐ QUICKDRAW	☐ HARNESS

CLIMB PARTNER(S)

MILESTONES ACHIEVED	AIMS FOR NEXT CLIMB

ROUTE TAKEN	BETA NOTES

FURTHER OBSERVATIONS

_____
_____
_____

LOCATION		DATE
CLIMB TYPE		
CLIMB HEIGHT		/ /

TEMPERATURE		DIFFICULTY RATING	1	2	3	4	5
HUMIDITY							
WEATHER CONDITION	☀ ☁ ❄ ⛈ 〰	TIME OF YEAR	🌷 ☀ 🍃 ❄				

START TIME	🕐	CLIMB CHECKLIST	
END TIME		☐ CLIMB ROPE	☐ CARABINER
TOTAL TIME TO TOP	⬆	☐ BELAY DEVICE	☐ HELMET
		☐ QUICKDRAW	☐ HARNESS

CLIMB PARTNER(S)

MILESTONES ACHIEVED	AIMS FOR NEXT CLIMB

ROUTE TAKEN	BETA NOTES

FURTHER OBSERVATIONS

_____
_____
_____

LOCATION		DATE	
CLIMB TYPE			
CLIMB HEIGHT		/ /	

TEMPERATURE		DIFFICULTY RATING	1	2	3	4	5
HUMIDITY							

WEATHER CONDITION	☀ ☁ ❄ ⚡ 〜	TIME OF YEAR	🌷 ☀ 🍁 ❄

START TIME	🕐	CLIMB CHECKLIST	
END TIME		☐ CLIMB ROPE	☐ CARABINER
TOTAL TIME TO TOP	⬆	☐ BELAY DEVICE	☐ HELMET
		☐ QUICKDRAW	☐ HARNESS

CLIMB PARTNER(S)

MILESTONES ACHIEVED	AIMS FOR NEXT CLIMB

ROUTE TAKEN	BETA NOTES

FURTHER OBSERVATIONS

LOCATION		DATE				
CLIMB TYPE		/ /				
CLIMB HEIGHT						
TEMPERATURE		DIFFICULTY RATING	1	2	3	4	5
HUMIDITY						
WEATHER CONDITION	☀ ☔ ❄ ⛈ 💨	TIME OF YEAR	🌷 ☀ 🍃 ❄			

START TIME		**CLIMB CHECKLIST**	
END TIME	🕐	☐ CLIMB ROPE	☐ CARABINER
TOTAL TIME TO TOP	⬆	☐ BELAY DEVICE	☐ HELMET
		☐ QUICKDRAW	☐ HARNESS

CLIMB PARTNER(S)

MILESTONES ACHIEVED	AIMS FOR NEXT CLIMB

ROUTE TAKEN	BETA NOTES

FURTHER OBSERVATIONS

LOCATION		DATE			
CLIMB TYPE					
CLIMB HEIGHT		/ /			

TEMPERATURE		DIFFICULTY RATING	1	2	3	4	5
HUMIDITY							

WEATHER CONDITION	☀ ☁ ❄ ⛈ 💨	TIME OF YEAR	🌷 ☀ 🍃 ❄

START TIME	🕐		**CLIMB CHECKLIST**	
END TIME			☐ CLIMB ROPE	☐ CARABINER
TOTAL TIME TO TOP	⬆		☐ BELAY DEVICE	☐ HELMET
			☐ QUICKDRAW	☐ HARNESS

CLIMB PARTNER(S)

MILESTONES ACHIEVED	AIMS FOR NEXT CLIMB

ROUTE TAKEN	BETA NOTES

FURTHER OBSERVATIONS

LOCATION		DATE		
CLIMB TYPE		/ /		
CLIMB HEIGHT				

TEMPERATURE		DIFFICULTY RATING	1 2 3 4 5
HUMIDITY			

WEATHER CONDITION	☀ ☁ ❄ ⛈ 🌬	TIME OF YEAR	🌷 ☀ 🍃 ❄

START TIME	🕐	**CLIMB CHECKLIST**	
END TIME		☐ CLIMB ROPE	☐ CARABINER
TOTAL TIME TO TOP	⬆	☐ BELAY DEVICE	☐ HELMET
		☐ QUICKDRAW	☐ HARNESS

CLIMB PARTNER(S)

MILESTONES ACHIEVED	AIMS FOR NEXT CLIMB

ROUTE TAKEN	BETA NOTES

FURTHER OBSERVATIONS

LOCATION		DATE	
CLIMB TYPE			
CLIMB HEIGHT		/ /	

TEMPERATURE		DIFFICULTY RATING	1 2 3 4 5
HUMIDITY			

WEATHER CONDITION	☀ ☁ ❄ ⛈ 🌬	TIME OF YEAR	🌷 ☀ 🍃 ❄

START TIME		CLIMB CHECKLIST	
END TIME		☐ CLIMB ROPE	☐ CARABINER
TOTAL TIME TO TOP	⬆	☐ BELAY DEVICE	☐ HELMET
		☐ QUICKDRAW	☐ HARNESS

CLIMB PARTNER(S)

MILESTONES ACHIEVED	AIMS FOR NEXT CLIMB

ROUTE TAKEN	BETA NOTES

FURTHER OBSERVATIONS

LOCATION		DATE		
CLIMB TYPE		/ /		
CLIMB HEIGHT				

TEMPERATURE		DIFFICULTY RATING	1 2 3 4 5
HUMIDITY			
WEATHER CONDITION	☀ ☁ ❄ ⛈ 💨	TIME OF YEAR	🌷 ☀ 🍃 ❄

START TIME	🕐	CLIMB CHECKLIST	
END TIME		☐ CLIMB ROPE	☐ CARABINER
TOTAL TIME TO TOP	⬆	☐ BELAY DEVICE	☐ HELMET
		☐ QUICKDRAW	☐ HARNESS

CLIMB PARTNER(S)

MILESTONES ACHIEVED | AIMS FOR NEXT CLIMB

ROUTE TAKEN | BETA NOTES

FURTHER OBSERVATIONS

___
___
___

LOCATION		DATE	
CLIMB TYPE			
CLIMB HEIGHT		/ /	

TEMPERATURE		DIFFICULTY RATING	1	2	3	4	5
HUMIDITY							

WEATHER CONDITION	☀ ☔ ❄ ⛈ 🌬	TIME OF YEAR	🌷 ☀ 🍃 ❄

START TIME	🕐	CLIMB CHECKLIST	
END TIME		☐ CLIMB ROPE	☐ CARABINER
TOTAL TIME TO TOP	⬆	☐ BELAY DEVICE	☐ HELMET
		☐ QUICKDRAW	☐ HARNESS

CLIMB PARTNER(S)

MILESTONES ACHIEVED | AIMS FOR NEXT CLIMB

ROUTE TAKEN | BETA NOTES

FURTHER OBSERVATIONS

LOCATION		DATE
CLIMB TYPE		
CLIMB HEIGHT		/ /

TEMPERATURE		DIFFICULTY RATING	1 2 3 4 5
HUMIDITY			

WEATHER CONDITION	☀ ☂ ❄ ⛈ 🌬	TIME OF YEAR	🌷 ☀ 🍃 ❄

START TIME	🕐	**CLIMB CHECKLIST**	
END TIME		☐ CLIMB ROPE	☐ CARABINER
TOTAL TIME TO TOP	⬆	☐ BELAY DEVICE	☐ HELMET
		☐ QUICKDRAW	☐ HARNESS

CLIMB PARTNER(S)

MILESTONES ACHIEVED	AIMS FOR NEXT CLIMB

ROUTE TAKEN	BETA NOTES

FURTHER OBSERVATIONS

LOCATION		DATE			
CLIMB TYPE					
CLIMB HEIGHT		/ /			

TEMPERATURE		DIFFICULTY RATING	1	2	3	4	5
HUMIDITY							

WEATHER CONDITION	☀ ☁ ❄ ⛈ 💨	TIME OF YEAR	🌷 ☀ 🍃 ❄

START TIME	🕐		CLIMB CHECKLIST	
END TIME			☐ CLIMB ROPE	☐ CARABINER
TOTAL TIME TO TOP	⬆		☐ BELAY DEVICE	☐ HELMET
			☐ QUICKDRAW	☐ HARNESS

CLIMB PARTNER(S)

MILESTONES ACHIEVED	AIMS FOR NEXT CLIMB

ROUTE TAKEN	BETA NOTES

FURTHER OBSERVATIONS

LOCATION		DATE		
CLIMB TYPE				
CLIMB HEIGHT		/ /		

TEMPERATURE		DIFFICULTY RATING	1	2	3	4	5
HUMIDITY						

WEATHER CONDITION	☀ ☁ ❄ ⛈ 💨	TIME OF YEAR	🌷 ☀ 🍃 ❄

START TIME	🕐	**CLIMB CHECKLIST**	
END TIME		☐ CLIMB ROPE	☐ CARABINER
TOTAL TIME TO TOP	⬆	☐ BELAY DEVICE	☐ HELMET
		☐ QUICKDRAW	☐ HARNESS

CLIMB PARTNER(S)

MILESTONES ACHIEVED	AIMS FOR NEXT CLIMB

ROUTE TAKEN	BETA NOTES

FURTHER OBSERVATIONS

LOCATION		DATE	
CLIMB TYPE			
CLIMB HEIGHT		/ /	

TEMPERATURE		DIFFICULTY RATING	1 2 3 4 5
HUMIDITY			
WEATHER CONDITION	☀ ☂ ❄ ⛈ 🌬	TIME OF YEAR	🌷 ☀ 🍁 ❄

START TIME	🕐	CLIMB CHECKLIST	
END TIME		☐ CLIMB ROPE	☐ CARABINER
TOTAL TIME TO TOP	⬆	☐ BELAY DEVICE	☐ HELMET
		☐ QUICKDRAW	☐ HARNESS

CLIMB PARTNER(S)

MILESTONES ACHIEVED	AIMS FOR NEXT CLIMB

ROUTE TAKEN	BETA NOTES

FURTHER OBSERVATIONS

LOCATION		DATE		
CLIMB TYPE				
CLIMB HEIGHT		/ /		

TEMPERATURE		DIFFICULTY RATING	1 2 3 4 5
HUMIDITY			

WEATHER CONDITION	☀ ☁ ❄ ⛈ 💨	TIME OF YEAR	🌷 ☀ 🍁 ❄

START TIME	🕐	CLIMB CHECKLIST	
END TIME		☐ CLIMB ROPE	☐ CARABINER
TOTAL TIME TO TOP	⬆	☐ BELAY DEVICE	☐ HELMET
		☐ QUICKDRAW	☐ HARNESS

CLIMB PARTNER(S)

MILESTONES ACHIEVED	AIMS FOR NEXT CLIMB

ROUTE TAKEN	BETA NOTES

FURTHER OBSERVATIONS

_____
_____
_____

LOCATION		DATE		
CLIMB TYPE				
CLIMB HEIGHT		/ /		

TEMPERATURE		DIFFICULTY RATING	1 2 3 4 5
HUMIDITY			
WEATHER CONDITION	☀ 🌧 ❄ ⛈ 💨	TIME OF YEAR	🌷 ☀ 🍂 ❄

START TIME		CLIMB CHECKLIST	
END TIME		☐ CLIMB ROPE	☐ CARABINER
		☐ BELAY DEVICE	☐ HELMET
TOTAL TIME TO TOP	↑	☐ QUICKDRAW	☐ HARNESS

CLIMB PARTNER(S)

MILESTONES ACHIEVED | AIMS FOR NEXT CLIMB

ROUTE TAKEN | BETA NOTES

FURTHER OBSERVATIONS

LOCATION		DATE
CLIMB TYPE		
CLIMB HEIGHT		/ /

TEMPERATURE		DIFFICULTY RATING	1 2 3 4 5
HUMIDITY			
WEATHER CONDITION	☀ ☁ ❄ ⛈ 🌬	TIME OF YEAR	🌷 ☀ 🍁 ❄

START TIME	🕐	**CLIMB CHECKLIST**	
END TIME		☐ CLIMB ROPE	☐ CARABINER
TOTAL TIME TO TOP	⬆	☐ BELAY DEVICE	☐ HELMET
		☐ QUICKDRAW	☐ HARNESS

CLIMB PARTNER(S)

MILESTONES ACHIEVED	AIMS FOR NEXT CLIMB

ROUTE TAKEN	BETA NOTES

FURTHER OBSERVATIONS

Thanks For Reading!

Just a quick message to thank you so much for picking up one of our books! Our sincere hope is that this book has given you the value we always look to provide, and hope we can continue to produce quality books that will in anyway contribute to a better quality of life for our readers.

We are a small independent publisher based in London, UK and we work with talented authors from around the world, who dedicate every ounce of their effort to craft these memorable books for your reading pleasure.

The author of this title would love to hear about your experience with the book, and your review will go a long way to provide them with the insight and encouragement they need to keep creating the kind of books you want to read.

Your Opinion Makes a Real Difference.

If you want to let us know what you thought about the book, please visit the Amazon website and give us your review. We read every single review, no matter how long or short!

Thanks again and until the next time....

HAPPY READING!

Copyright © 2021 - Buy The Bay Books

Printed in Great Britain
by Amazon